The Wild West in American History

SOLDIERS

Written by Leonard J. Matthews
Illustrated by Geoffrey Campion and others

Library of Congress Cataloging-in-Publication Data

Matthews, Leonard, 1920-
 Soldiers / by Leonard Matthews.

   p. cm. — (The Wild West in American history)
  Summary: Relates some of the battles between the United States
Army and North American Indians in the West during the nineteenth
century.
  ISBN 0-86625-365-3
  1. Indians of North America — West (U.S.) — Wars — Juvenile
literature. 2. United States. Army — History — Juvenile literature.
[1. Indians of North American — West (U.S.) — Wars. 2. United States.
Army — History.] I. Title. II. Series.
E78.W5M33 1988   88-3948
978'.00497 - dc19   CIP
                                                     AC

Rourke Publications, Inc.
Vero Beach, Florida 32964

SOLDIERS

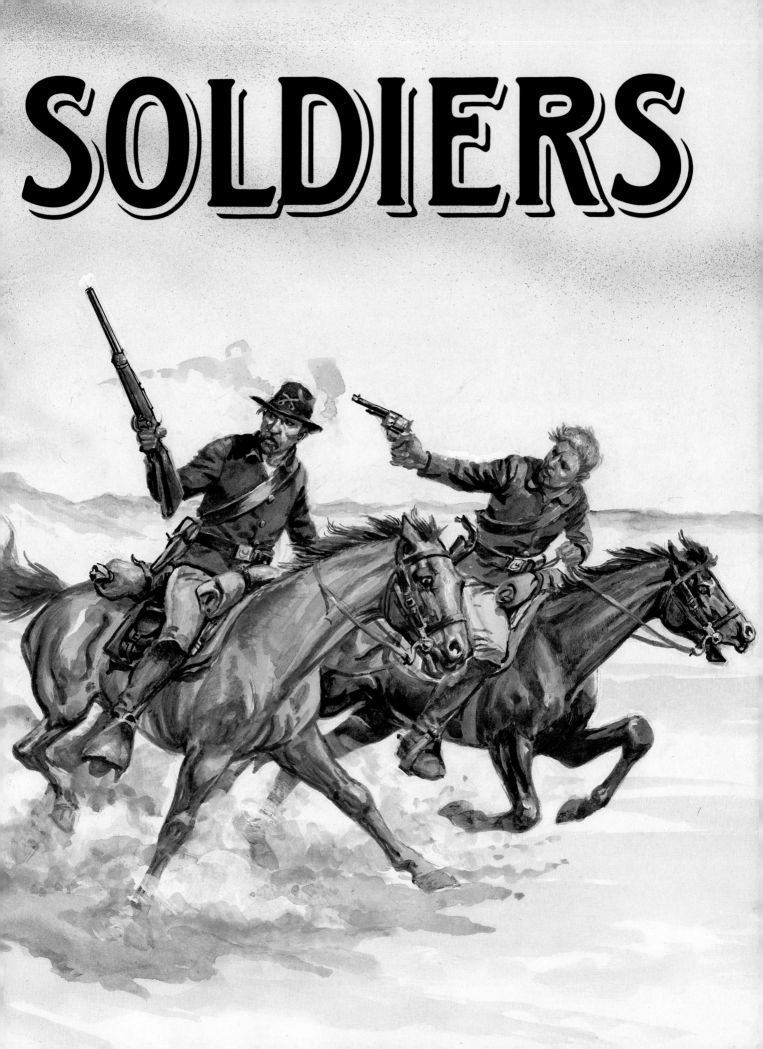

SOLDIERS

When the Indians of the American West went on the warpath against the white men, the task of subduing the warring tribes fell to the United States Army. The role of the soldiers was similar to that of a police force. They were to protect the white settlers and try to bring about a peace between the white pioneers and the Indians.

At first, however, the soldiers were not prepared for the entirely new way of fighting that faced them. They were used to fighting against men who were trained in regular army warfare. Their new enemies were tough, ferocious guerrilla fighters who swooped down on settlements in lightning raids, burning and killing. They appeared suddenly out of nowhere to attack wagon trains and stagecoaches. They had mastered the art of hit-and-run tactics. Being superb horsemen, they made their getaway at speed, leaving lookouts posted along their trail to deal with any pursuing soldiers. They broke up into small parties, covering their tracks so thoroughly that cavalry detachments frequently found the chase hopeless.

When the American Civil War between the North and South ended in 1865, the United States Army was greatly reduced in numbers. As a result, the soldiers who fought in the Indian wars often found themselves outnumbered and up against appalling odds.

In the end, though, they defeated the Indians in December 1890. The victorious army had complete control over the West, and the defeated Indians lost their freedom, their lands, and their way of life.

The story that follows relates to some of the United States Army's battles against its daunting Native American enemies.

TREACHERY IN APACHE PASS

Second Lieutenant George N. Bascom rode at the head of a platoon of infantry who were mounted on mules. As he headed for Apache Pass in the Dragoon Mountains in Arizona, he knew little of what was to come. Within a short time, he would be responsible for starting a terrible war of vengeance and bloodshed. It was to last for eleven years and would cost the Americans hundreds of lives.

George Bascom was a young, inexperienced officer. He was fresh from West Point Military Academy, and he knew nothing about Indians. He did not know the difference between an outlaw Indian and a chieftain. To him all Indians were alike. He was soon to learn differently.

Cochise was Chief of the Chiricahua (Cheer-a-KA-wa) Apaches. He was an intelligent and wise leader, and a strong, powerfully built man. He was friendly with the whites who came to his territory, and those who knew him respected and liked him. Cochise allowed them to run a stagecoach line through Apache Pass. To protect the stagecoaches his warriors guarded the pass against renegade Apache bands who were not of his tribe. He also supplied wood for the stage station in the middle of the pass.

This was the peaceful situation between Cochise and the whites until January 1861, when Bascom was sent to question Cochise

Lieutenant Bascomb led his men through Apache Pass watched by Apache scouts.

about the kidnapping of a white boy.

A renegade band of Apaches had raided a ranch belonging to a settler named John Ward. They had run off with his cattle and had also taken his stepson. Ward reported the incident to the commanding officer of the nearest army post. He blamed Cochise, whom he did not know, for the raid, because he knew Cochise's warriors were in the area. The fort commander tried to convince Ward that Cochise was peaceful and friendly and would not have done such a thing. But Ward would not listen, and he insisted that the Apache chief be brought in for questioning. Had a more experienced officer, instead of Bascom, been sent to bring Cochise in, the history of Arizona might well have been very different.

Lieutenant Bascom went straight through Apache Pass. That showed how inexperienced he was, because if Cochise had been responsible for the raid on Ward's ranch, it would have meant that he was hostile. And if he were hostile, he could easily have attacked Bascom in the pass. Bascom believed him to be hostile, yet he led his men into the pass without first sending out scouts to make sure it was safe. The pass was a deep, narrow canyon through the mountains, a real deathtrap where hostile Apaches could have wiped out his force in a matter of minutes. Luckily for him and his platoon, Cochise was friendly. Bascom and his men rode safely through to the stage station.

The stationmaster did his best to make Bascom realize he was making a big mistake in assuming that Cochise was guilty of the raid. But Bascom preferred to accept Ward's accusation.

Cochise was invited to Bascom's tent under a white flag of peace. He took several of his people with him. Through an interpreter, Bascom accused Cochise of raiding Ward's ranch and demanded the return of the boy and the cattle.

The Apache chief realized that the young officer had much to learn. Through the interpreter, Cochise told Bascom that because he was new to Apache country and did not understand the ways of his people, he would overlook the insult of accusing him of the raid. He offered Bascom his hand in friendship and said he would find out which Apache band had stolen the boy and the cattle. Cochise promised he would do all he could to see that they were returned to Ward.

Bascom was furious that Cochise had dared to speak to him as an equal. Angrily he told the chief that he would hold him and his companions prisoner until the Ward boy was found. Ordering his sergeant to arrest the Apaches, he turned his back on Cochise and stalked out of the tent.

A sudden, dangerous glint shone in the eyes of Cochise, and a look of pure hatred spread across his handsome face. No man insulted the chief of the Chiricahua Apaches.

In a lightning move he whipped out his knife, slashed the back of the tent and escaped before the startled soldiers standing outside realized what was happening. By the time they fired after him he was well away. A stray bullet hit him in the leg, but he managed to reach the rocky path leading up to his camp.

Bascom, now more angry than ever over the escape of Cochise, gave orders for the other Apaches to be taken prisoner.

APACHE VENGEANCE

*M*ost of the infantrymen under Bascom's command were worried at his treatment of Cochise. His sergeant warned him that a full-scale war could follow if he did not release the remaining Apaches. Bascom's pride though, would not let him take the advice of men more experienced in the ways of the Apaches, and he refused.

Cochise, in his anger, called the entire Apache nation to war. He told the chiefs of the other Apache tribes that the days of friendship with the whites had ended because of the treachery of the lieutenant.

He captured three whites and held them hostage. He offered to exchange them for the Apaches who were being held prisoner, but Bascom would not agree. He told Cochise to return the Ward boy. Only then would Bascom release the Apaches.

Cochise's warriors lost no time in going on

Lieutenant George N. Bascomb

the warpath. They attacked a stagecoach and killed the teamsters. Then they ran off a herd of cattle being watered at a spring near the stage station, killing a white man and wounding two more. During this attack some Indians were killed.

The deaths of his warriors aroused the fury of Cochise even more, and he killed the three white men he had been holding hostage, together with the stationmaster.

In retaliation, the Apaches held by Bascom were hanged. Cochise assumed that it was the lieutenant who gave the order to hang them. In fact it was not Bascom, but a Doctor Irwin, who had brought medical supplies to Bascom's camp. Bascom had protested against the hanging. He was beginning to realize that an Indian uprising was about to take place.

In the years that followed, Cochise waged a relentless battle against the whites in Arizona, New Mexico, and across the border into Mexico. Many hundreds of soldiers and settlers were killed.

The United States Army sent thousands of soldiers, infantry, and cavalry to the Southwest to try to capture Cochise. The troops were load- ed down with equipment, food, and supplies. They were no match for the Apaches who made lightning attacks then rapidly disappeared into the rocky wilderness of the mountains, leaving no trails behind them. To confuse the soldiers, they attacked in several places at the same time.

The Apaches were living up to their name, which means "enemy." The army had never come up against such a cunning and deadly foe.

The U.S. government was alarmed, because the Apaches were having everything their own way. Some of the finest, most courageous officers, who thought they knew the ways of Indian fighting, were powerless to stop the warring Apaches. Government troops were continually on the move but were unable to make any headway. They tried many times to get Cochise to come to terms, but he refused to meet any high-ranking officers. After the behavior of Bascom, he suspected treachery and no longer trusted them.

THE WAR DRUMS CEASE

*P*resident Grant gave General O.O. Howard the job of trying to find a peaceful solution to the Indian problems of the Southwest.

It was a good move. General Howard was a fine man. He felt sorry for the Indian tribes, who had been so disgracefully treated by his government. He wanted more than anything to end the terrible war between his people and the Apaches. He felt that if only he could talk to Cochise, the chief might be willing to come to terms.

Reaching Cochise was the problem. Luck, however, was with Howard. In New Mexico he met a white man, Tom Jeffords, who was not only a friend of Cochise but was his blood-brother. General Howard explained to Jeffords that it was his job to end the bloodshed that had lasted for eleven years. Would Jeffords take him to Cochise so that he could talk to him?

Jeffords agreed but he could only guarantee Howard's safety if he would go with him alone. Cochise would not let the general into his stronghold if he had soldiers with him.

Howard trusted Jeffords and promised to leave his army escort behind. They set off to journey the several hundred miles to Arizona with two Apache guides, friends of Jeffords. One was a nephew of Cochise, and the other was the son of an old friend of the chief. On reaching Arizona, the guides sent up smoke

Tom Jeffords was not only a friend of Cochise, the Apache chieftain, he was also the Indian's blood-brother. Tom knew he would be welcome in Cochise's camp.

signals to warn all Apaches that the four men were headed for Cochise's stronghold and were friends.

Arriving at last in the foothills of the Dragoon Mountains, they were met by two of Cochise's warriors and escorted to his camp high up in the mountains.

General Howard waited patiently while Jeffords and Cochise greeted each other. After the greetings were over, Jeffords, who spoke the Apache language, introduced Cochise to Howard, telling him he could trust the general who had been sent by the Great Father in Washington to make peace between the Apaches and the white people.

A warm smile touched Cochise's mouth as he shook hands with the general and welcomed him to his lodge.

As Howard looked at the friendly, open-faced man before him, he found it hard to connect him with all the terrible Apache raids. He saw a man of intelligence and strong character, not a savage. Howard could not help but like Cochise.

Cochise admitted that he wanted peace more than anything, and that it was not he who had broken it in the first place.

Howard assured the chieftain that this time the President of the United States really wished to have a lasting peace with the Chiricahua Apaches.

After a lot of discussion, Cochise came to terms with the general. There would be no more fighting on either side. He insisted that the Chiricahua reservation should include the mountains and valleys of his tribe's homeland. Any other climate might affect the health of his people and eventually kill them, and he would not allow that to happen. He also insisted that Tom Jeffords be appointed the Apache Indian Agent. Jeffords did not want the job, but he could not let his friend down. For the sake of peace, he reluctantly agreed.

General Howard happily agreed to the Chief's reasonable demands. He had done what he had set out to do; he had ended the long Apache war.

Cochise kept the terms of peace until his death on June 8, 1874.

As for Lieutenant Bascom, he was killed a year after his meeting with Cochise. He died, not at the hands of Apaches, but during a battle in New Mexico between the Union and Con- **federate troops. The Civil War had spread to the Southwest.**

Mickey Free, the army scout.

THE KIDNAPPED BOY

The boy who was kidnapped by a band of Apaches was never returned to his stepfather, John Ward. His name was Felix Telles, and he was about twelve years old when he was snatched from his home. He spent his boyhood with the Apaches. Eventually he gained his freedom and became an army scout. For some unknown reason, he decided to use the name Mickey Free.

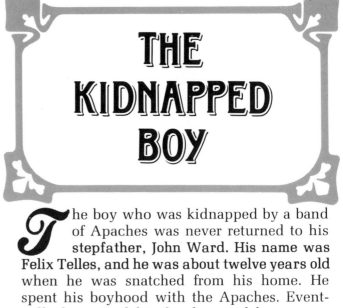

Because his kidnapping had led to eleven years of war between the whites and the Apaches, he was blamed and hated by the Indians. Such feelings were unfair on the part of the Apaches, because it was not the boy's fault that he had been kidnapped and that war had resulted.

The feeling was mutual, though. Mickey hated the Apaches, and it is said that he did all he could to stir up trouble for them. Because he could speak English as well as Apache, he was used as an army interpreter until the chiefs found out that he was twisting their words, making it impossible at times for them to reach terms. Once they discovered his treachery they refused to speak through him and insisted on their own interpreters.

Although the whites found him reliable, not many of the army scouts liked him any more than the Apaches did.

It would seem that Mickey Free did not have a happy life.

The year was 1868 and the frontier was in the grip of a vengeance war. Several battles took place between Indians and the U.S. Cavalry.

THE VALIANT VOLUNTEERS

General Philip Sheridan was frustrated and angered by the guerrilla tactics of the Plains Indians.

It was 1868 and the frontier was in the grip of a vengeance war. The Cheyennes and their allies, the Sioux and the Arapahos, were on the rampage, killing, raiding, and plundering. No army patrol, no homestead, no white settlement was safe from the fury of the warriors.

General Sheridan was in charge of the Indian campaign that covered more than a million square miles of frontier country. This area was the home of some 192,000 Indians. Sheridan

was worried, because he had an insufficient number of trained soldiers to hold the Indians in check. Seventy-six army posts and camps were spread over the territory, but Sheridan needed more cavalry and infantry regiments to man the garrisons. Only if he got these men could he hope to subdue the warriors of the ninety-nine tribes who were on the warpath.

The General's aide-de-camp, Major George Forsyth, known to his fellow officers as Sandy, suggested a solution.

He believed that the army had been using the wrong tactics to fight the Indians. He thought that a small, highly mobile force of men who traveled light and fast would be far more effective than large forces of troops slowed down by cumbersome supply wagons. These small forces could track down the Indians and make them fight.

Sandy Forsyth had risen from a private of dragoons to brevet brigadier general in the Civil War. He was the trusted aide of General Sheridan, the Union Army Cavalry hero. At the end of the war Forsyth had willingly given up his high rank and reverted back to major in order to join the Indian-Fighting Army and be again under the command of Sheridan.

Major Sandy Forsyth gathered together a troop of fifty tough volunteers, mostly veterans of the Civil War.

General Sheridan knew of Forsyth's distinguished gallantry during the war and considered him an excellent officer. General Sheridan was impressed by his suggestion and told him to organize a troop of fifty volunteers without delay.

Major Forsyth quickly gathered his troop of volunteers together. His second in command was First Lieutenant Fred H. Beecher. Another soldier, General William H.H. McCall, was so anxious to see action that he took the much-reduced rank of sergeant in order to ride with Forsyth. All fifty volunteers were men of outstanding courage, mostly veterans of the Civil War. They were ready and willing to risk their lives in subduing the warring Indians.

Early one morning in late August of 1868, the intrepid little troop rode out from Fort Hayes, complete with a pack train of four mules carrying ammunition and medical supplies. Each man was armed with a seven shot Spencer repeating rifle and an army model Colt revolver. They were on the track of

a band of Indians who had attacked a freight wagon near the western terminus of the Kansas Pacific railroad. The wagon drivers had been killed in the attack.

During the days of hard riding that followed, Forsyth and his men kept losing and then picking up the trail of a fairly large war party. The trail eventually brought them close to the favorite camping grounds of the Cheyenne, Sioux, and Arapahos in Colorado.

On the afternoon of September 16, their scout, Abner "Sharp" Grover, spotted recent tracks of another large band of warriors in a valley at the fork of the Arikaree and Republican Rivers. These warriors appeared to have joined forces with the war party Forsyth and his men had been trailing.

The Major decided that the valley was a good spot to make camp since there was a small brush-covered island in the middle of the river bed that would provide an excellent defensive position if it were needed. He planned to rest that night and attack the warriors' camp the next morning. He knew that Indians seldom attacked at night and did not think that he and his men had been detected by the Indians, but he took no chances. He posted sentries, had the

The alarm was raised at dawn and the sleeping soldiers were soon roused. Quickly they grabbed their guns.

men tether their horses and pack mules securely, and told them to keep their rifles beside them when they bedded down.

But the Indians had spotted them. At dawn the following day, 600 war-painted warriors were poised on the hills overlooking the soldiers' camp, ready to attack.

Fortunately for Forsyth and his men, the surprise attack was spoiled by some overeager young warriors who swooped down on the camp uttering hideous war cries in an attempt to stampede the soldiers' horses. Their attempt failed, since the mounts had been securely tethered, and the sentries managed to turn them back. The noise roused the camp, and the soldiers hurriedly saddled their mounts and grabbed their rifles.

For one terrifying moment, the soldiers stood rooted to the ground with fear as they looked up in the early morning light and saw the huge war party towering above them. Warriors and ponies were daubed with war paint. The experienced warriors with battle honors wore their prized warbonnets and war shirts, while the rest were stripped down to breechclouts. Lances, bows, tomahawks, and rifles were held motionless above their heads while they waited the command to attack. It came seconds later, a terrible blood-curdling war whoop from the six hundred throats in unison.

Major Forsyth yelled the order for carbines at the ready. As the whooping Indians raced down on the little band of men, he gave the command to fire. The concentrated fire from the Spencers slowed down the charge momentarily, because the Indians had not expected such a barrage of bullets. In that brief respite, Forsyth ordered his men to mount and ride for the island.

The soldiers made for the island, the war-cries of the Indians ringing in their ears.

THE BATTLE OF BEECHER'S ISLAND

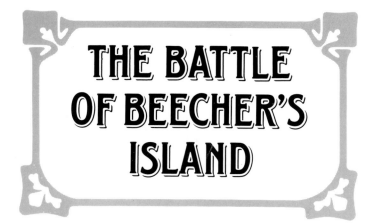

The little island was in the center of the river about 75 yards from the bank. Because of a dry summer, the river was only a few inches deep. Amid the wild yells of the Indians milling around to attack, the soldiers raced towards the island, without stopping to take their food, provisions, or medical supplies.

Gaining the island, they formed a circle with their mounts, which they tied to the bushes. Forsyth, Beecher, McCall, and Grover flung themselves down in the long grass, and kept up a steady fire. Meanwhile the rest of the party began frantically scooping out the sandy soil to dig rifle pits large enough to protect their bodies from the flying bullets.

The enemy seemed to be everywhere, firing as they charged the island in an attempt to kill the soldiers at close quarters. Under Forsyth's orders, a hail of bullets from the soldier's repeating rifles broke the wall of mounted warriors. They were forced to part and gallop down both sides of the island and beyond it.

The Indians regrouped and charged. Again they were driven back by the devastating fire from the Spencers. Although Forsyth was hit in the first violent attack, he calmed and encouraged his men. All their horses had been killed, and for added protection the soldiers used them to barricade their rifle pits.

The fight was just beginning. Sitting on the crest of the hill overlooking the small island was one of the great Cheyenne warriors. He was tall, handsome, and muscular. Known as Bat to his tribe and his enemies, he was called Roman Nose by white settlers and soldiers because his nose was hooked.

The Cheyennes believed that this famous warrior had a charmed life, since the arrows and bullets never touched him. He could ride through heavy fire without being hit. Roman Nose believed that his protection came from his sacred warbonnet, which he always wore in battle. The power of the headdress, however, depended on his obeying certain taboos. If disregarded, these taboos could take away the warbonnet's protective powers.

The night before the battle, Roman Nose had unknowingly violated one of the taboos. There had been no time for a ceremony of purification to restore the protective power to the warbonnet. One taboo was not to eat any food prepared or touched by an iron instrument. He had been invited by the Sioux to a feast, and too late he found out that the squaw who had cooked the meal had used an iron fork. He knew that if he donned his warbonnet and entered the fight, he would be killed. But he was a fighting chief of great courage; he would lead his warriors in the next attack.

And so it was that the mighty Roman Nose, mounted on a huge chestnut war pony, took his place at the head of his warriors. He wore his magnificent plumed warbonnet and brandished a rifle over his head. With a deep-throated battle cry, followed by a roar from hundreds of Indians, he led the massed warriors in a death-defying charge.

Fear gripped the little band of soldiers as they saw the formidable enemy charging down on them from all sides. They had recognized Roman Nose, but they remained steady and waited until the Indians were fifty yards away before opening fire.

At Forsyth's command, the soldiers fired as one man. A wall of bullets smashed into the Indians, downing men and horses. But the waves of Indians kept coming. A second volley poured from the Spencers, then a third, and a fourth. As the riders and horses fell, those behind leapt over them. A fifth volley brought gaps in the Indians' ranks, and their horses floundered in the water. Roman Nose, the plumes of his warbonnet streaming out behind him, led his warriors closer and closer to the sweating soldiers, whose repeaters were pouring bullet after bullet into the charging Indians.

Forsyth was hit again and so was Lt. Beecher and the surgeon, Dr. Mooers. But the gallant soldiers never faltered. Forsyth looked up through pain-filled eyes and saw that Roman Nose was only ten yards away. Then suddenly it happened. A bullet from one of the soldier's Spencers smashed into him, and the mighty warrior and his mount crashed down in the shallow, muddy water. The medicine of Roman Nose was broken forever.

Forsyth's men remained steady and waited calmly for their leader to give the signal before opening fire.

As the soldiers watched, the startled Indians faltered and reined in their mounts. Those closest to their dead war chief dragged him out of the water and carried him away, while the others fired half-hearted volleys at the white men. They then veered round and rode off in confusion and despair. With no Roman Nose to lead them, all fight went out of the Indians.

Abner "Sharp" Grover said it was the most violent Indian attack he had ever experienced. Seven soldiers were dead, including Lt. Beecher and Dr. Mooers, and sixteen had been wounded. Forsyth had been shot in the thigh, his left leg was broken below the knee, and he had a bullet wound in his head.

The Indians did not charge again, but they kept the soldiers under siege with long-range sniping. Forsyth asked for four volunteers to try to get help from Fort Wallace, about 10 miles away. The soldiers had to sneak through the Indian lines. Then to avoid any Indian scouts, they walked on foot by night and rested by day. They set off in pairs within two days of each other.

The besieged troop knew that if one of the four men was able to reach Fort Wallace, it would be well over a week before help could arrive. With four able-bodied men gone, the little band was almost defenseless. Major Forsyth urged those who were not wounded to try to get away, but they would not desert their gallant commander or their comrades.

Sandy Forsyth was in such agony with his thigh he was forced to cut out the bullet himself with his knife, gritting his teeth against the terrible pain.

On the hilltop, the Indians were waiting and watching for the soldiers to die, either from their wounds or from starvation. Had they attacked again the soldiers could not have held them off. But the warriors were so stunned by the death of Roman Nose they had no wish to continue the fight.

The soldiers held on with grim determination. Somehow they had to stay alive. They had no food and existed on a few berries and rotting horseflesh, which they seasoned with gunpowder to try to make it edible.

Nine days later Abner "Sharp" Grover, who was acting sentry, let out a hoarse cry. Reinforcements had arrived. All four soldiers had made it to Fort Wallace. Captain Louis H. Carpenter rode in with two troops of the 10th Cavalry just in time to save Forsyth and his men. The 10th Cavalry was one of four black regiments that fought in the Indian wars.

Major Forsyth and his men decided to name the island after young Lt. Beecher, who had been the first to die during the battle.

Forsyth's idea of a small band of mobile men did not turn out to be the solution he envisioned. They did not conquer the warring Indians, but at least he and his troop of valiant men had done their best in trying out the idea. They had been outnumbered twenty to one. Half their number had been killed or wounded, and they had been stranded without food and medical supplies, yet they had held the Indians at bay and had not surrendered.

The story of Forsyth and the Battle of Beecher's Island was told countless times in army posts and around campfires all across the

Led by Captain Louis H. Carpenter, two troops of the 10th Cavalry charged the Indians just in time to save Forsyth and his men. The Indians turned and fled.

Forsyth and his men were outnumbered twenty to one but they had not surrendered.

Plains. Newspapers across the country reported the heroic action.

The action itself was not significant as battles go. Incredibly, only nine Indians had been killed. There were many wounded, but it was the horses that were killed in great numbers. Yet the Battle of Beecher's Island was one of the most honored and glorified in the history of the Indian-Fighting Army.

TWO GALLANT MEN

On a hot June day in 1877, warriors of the Nez Perce tribe ambushed two troops of the 1st Cavalry in a canyon in Idaho.

The troopers were outnumbered eight to one. Their sergeant, Michael McCarthy, hurriedly called six of his men to follow him up a rocky slope. They dismounted, grabbed their repeating rifles, and poured rapid fire into the charging warriors.

The Indian attack was so fierce that the rest of the troopers were forced to retreat. Sergeant McCarthy and his men were left to fend for themselves. With Indian warriors swarming all around, uttering hideous war cries, the little band of cavalrymen somehow managed to mount up and fight their way through the yelling Indians. When their ammunition gave out, they used their rifle butts as clubs or slashed at the warriors with their knives.

Two troopers were killed, and the sergeant's horse was shot out from under him. He leapt on to a riderless horse but that, too, was killed. By this time McCarthy had become separated from his men. Horseless, he took refuge in a clump of bushes and laid low. Luck was with the remaining four troopers who raced to safety.

While waiting for a chance to escape, McCarthy saw a war party heading his way. At the same time he noticed, to his horror, that his boots were sticking out of the bush under which he was taking cover. To move his legs might attract the attention of the Indians. Instead he rapidly slipped off his boots, left them where they were and crawled deeper into the bushes.

He waited until nightfall. Then he crept into the hills and headed for his camp. Three days later, tired, hungry, and thirsty, with sore and bleeding feet, he reached his company. For his bravery in action, Sergeant McCarthy was awarded the Medal of Honor.

Only 416 soldiers won the army's highest award during all the years of the Indian-Fighting Army. No man above the rank of major was given this decoration, not even General George Armstrong Custer.

Another unsung hero who was awarded the Medal of Honor for valor was Private Jeremiah J. Murphy of the 3rd Cavalry.

It was March 1876, and the village of Crazy Horse, the mighty Sioux chieftain, was under attack.

Murphy, with five other soldiers, was ordered to form a picket line. The angry Sioux warriors immediately broke through the line,

The little band of cavalrymen mounted and fought their way through the howling Indians. McCarthy's horse was shot from under him and the sergeant fell headlong.

George Armstrong Custer, the long-haired young general as he looked during the Civil War, twelve years before his last battle.

and Murphy and his tiny force found themselves cut off from the rest of the column.

Valiantly the troopers tried to fight their way through the encircling Indians, but four were killed and one was badly wounded. Murphy was about to make a final run for safety when he heard the wounded soldier cry out to him to be saved.

As Murphy turned to hoist the wounded man onto his shoulder a bullet smashed the butt of his carbine. Facing a hail of bullets from the Sioux's rifles, he tried to run on foot for the shelter of some trees. But one of the bullets hit his wounded comrade and killed him.

Murphy laid him on the ground. Then before the warriors realized what he was up to, he raced through their ranks and managed to reach the column. Parts of his uniform were torn by bullet holes but, to the amazement of his company who had watched his dash to safety, he was unhurt.

The courageous young private deserved his Medal of Honor.

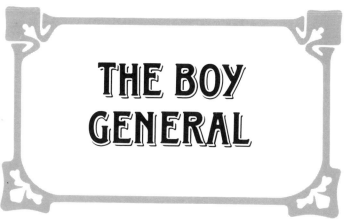

THE BOY GENERAL

*L*ieutenant Colonel George Armstrong Custer was making history when, riding at the head of the 7th Cavalry, he led his gallant regiment to the Battle of the Little Big Horn.

The intrepid officer wore a kerchief knotted casually at his neck and a broad-brimmed hat on his fair hair. He turned in his saddle, his eyes shining with pride as he looked back at his regiment.

The 7th Cavalry was made up of twelve troops. It was Custer's idea to have the horses of each troop of the same color, and the bays, sorrels, blacks, chestnuts, and greys made a colorful pattern as they trotted rhythmically along to the singing of "Garry Owen," the regimental battle song.

With standards and guidons fluttering proudly, six hundred men in army blue set out to fight over three thousand Sioux and Cheyenne warriors on the warpath. They were armed with carbines and revolvers. No saber scabbards hung against the yellow stripes of their blue breeches. Sabers had been ruled out as obsolete weapons. They were considered useless against bullets, and their clatter could betray a surprise attack.

Custer's men were armed only with single-shot Springfield rifles, while the Indians had repeating rifles which they bought from traders. Moreover the cartridge cases of the Springfields were soft and frequently stuck in the overheated breeches. If these facts worried the brilliant commander, his anxiety did not show in his face.

Forty percent of the regiment were recruits, and thirteen of his officers were detailed for other duties. Yet Custer had trained his men well. The 7th was considered one of the finest cavalry units in the United States, and he was confident it would stand up against any Indian attack. It had already done so many times since he had taken command.

George Armstrong Custer was an impetuous, glory-seeking cavalry officer. His career in the Civil War was outstanding, and at twenty-two he was a Major General. Because he was so young, he was referred to as the Boy General. He was utterly fearless and was commended for gallantry five times. At the end of the Civil War he joined the Indian-Fighting Army and was given command of the 7th Cavalry. Like all the high-ranking officers of the Civil War, he had to revert to a lower rank. He went in as a captain but was soon promoted to lieutenant-colonel. He was tall and handsome and wore his hair long. The Indians named him "Yellow Hair."

Custer was called "The Last of the Cavaliers" because of his love of pomp and ceremony, rolling drums, blaring trumpets and flashing sabers. He liked wearing fringed buckskins and rode thoroughbred Kentucky horses. Whenever possible, his big hunting dogs loped along on either side of his mount.

He was an impatient young man who hated following discipline but who was very strict in enforcing it on those under his command. His

Custer led his men out of Fort Lincoln determined to find and fight the Indians. Little did he know that three thousand Indians were waiting for him. Death, too, awaited him.

biggest fault was that he was overeager for action, and he was known several times to disobey orders. In fact, when he was not in the thick of a battle, he was in the thick of trouble. A cavalry brigade once mutinied under his harsh discipline and court-martials and warnings were common events in his career.

Custer never lost an opportunity to win glory, and call attention to himself. On one occasion, in 1878, he had trumped up an excuse for attacking a peaceful camp of Southern Cheyennes that had been set up, under their chief Black Kettle, on the banks of the Washita River.

He had convinced General Philip Sheridan that the Indians were about to take to the warpath, and Sheridan had ordered him to destroy the Cheyenne camp, kill all the warriors and ponies, and bring back the women and children as prisoners.

Custer carried out this merciless order to the letter. Cautiously he led the troopers through a snowstorm and arrived just outside the Cheyenne camp without being seen because of the blinding snow. Impatiently he waited throughout the long night and then, at dawn on a bitterly cold day, he attacked the sleeping camp. His cavalrymen slew more than a hundred warriors, including their chief, as well as many women and children whose lifeless bodies were never counted. Then they burned every lodge, slaughtered hundreds of ponies, and marched those few men, women, and children still left alive back through knee-deep snow to captivity.

Custer had noticed that a few Cheyennes had managed to make good their escape, so before leaving for Fort Dodge, he ordered Major Joel Elliott and eighteen troopers to pursue the lucky few and capture them. Unfortunately Elliott and his men were all slain by furious Indians from nearby encampments.

Impatiently, Custer waited throughout the long night. It was dawn when he ordered his men to attack the sleeping Cheyenne camp. His orders were to kill all the warriors and their ponies.

The men of the 7th Cavalry slew more than a hundred warriors as well as women and children.

Nevertheless, Custer reckoned he had won a great victory. In fact, he had signed his own death warrant. Eight years later, a combined force of Cheyennes and Sioux, all hungry for revenge, were to overwhelm him and his men on the banks of another river, one that is written large in the records of the 7th Cavalry — the Little Big Horn.

It was as the over-proud George Armstrong Custer led his regiment towards the scene of his last battle that he must have reminded himself of the fact that he had very nearly missed leading his regiment into action. He had offended President Grant by accusing his government of corruption. The angry President had forbidden him to take part in the expedition to the Little Big Horn, but Generals Sheridan and Terry had asked the President to reconsider his decision. At the last moment, Grant had given his permission for the reckless, courageous officer to rejoin his regiment.

And so it was that on that particular day in June 1876, this dashing cavalier of the Plains, riding a Kentucky thoroughbred named Vic, led his regiment to the junction of the Yellowstone and Rosebud Rivers. There on a supply ship called the "Far West," Custer met General Terry and Colonel Gibbon to draw up a final campaign of action against the Indians.

GLORY HUNTING

The Sioux and Cheyenne warriors had taken the warpath because the Sioux treaty had been broken. White settlers were flocking to their territory in the Black Hills in search of gold. The Indian could no longer depend upon the word of his white brother. His lands and his buffalo were being taken away from him, and the Indian had only one recourse: war. The warriors were under the leadership of Sitting Bull, Crazy Horse, Rain-in-the-Face, Gall, and other noted chiefs.

Custer's orders were to meet Terry's and Gibbon's troops on June 26 at a point on the Little Big Horn River. The three columns would then close in on the Sioux and bottle them up in the Little Big Horn Valley.

General Terry gave Custer definite instructions not to follow the Indian trail if it led to the valley of the Little Big Horn. He was to turn south and wait for the other two columns to join him, and only then the attack would commence.

Before the 7th Cavalry set off on the last trail, General Terry reviewed the troops. This time the band would not be playing them into battle, but the massed trumpeters blew a stirring march. Custer's own headquarters flag, red and blue with silver crossed sabers, flew alongside the regimental standard carried by the color sergeants. As Custer turned in his saddle to salute Terry and Gibbon, they wished him good luck and the Colonel called out: "Now, Custer, don't be greedy, but wait for us."

Custer shouted back as he waved: "No, I won't." Custer's reply, of course, could be taken either way. Did he mean that he would not be greedy for battle, or that he would not wait for the other two officers' troops to join him?

Custer pushed his men hard, riding thirty miles a day and sometimes more. The heat and the grueling pace caused blisters to form and split on the legs of the troopers. The horses began to suffer from sores caused by sweat under their saddles.

He advanced along an Indian trail leading west towards the Big Horn Mountains. His scouts reported hundreds of Indians on the move. When they reached the point where they were to wait for the troops of Terry and Gibbon, Custer's impatience got the better of him. He was early because he had imposed forced marches. Instead of waiting for the other officers and their men, he gave the signal "Forward, march."

He led his 7th down the broad trail toward the valley of the Little Big Horn, deliberately disobeying his general's orders. He saw before him the chance for a great victory, which would bring triumph and glory for himself and his regiment. He could not resist taking that chance.

Custer's rash action turned the Battle of the Little Big Horn into the greatest of all Indian victories and the worst of all army defeats at the hands of the Indians.

The 7th Cavalry with Custer in the lead took the broad trail towards the Little Big Horn River.

The 7th approached the fork of the Rosebud and Little Big Horn Rivers. In that Montana valley, unknown to Custer, was a village of ten thousand Sioux and Cheyennes, over three thousand of them fighting warriors. He and his six hundred men were surrounded by Indians who had closed in behind them.

Because he was ahead of schedule, help from Terry and Gibbon could not be expected for at least another day. His men and their horses were exhausted. Again and again his scouts warned him to turn back because there were too many Indians. Each time Custer retorted that there were not too many Indians on the whole of the North American continent for the 7th Cavalry to handle. In fact, the size of the Indian force made him more eager to fight. The greater the number he defeated, the greater would be the fame of his victory. Perhaps had he known that the strength of the Indian force was three thousand warriors, he might not have rushed so eagerly into battle.

The headstrong commander gave his officers their battle orders. He divided the regiment into three. Five troops, two hundred and eleven men, were to accompany him. Three

Quietly the Indians waited for the arrival of the doomed soldiers.

Custer's scout, Curley, a Crow Indian. It was he who took back the news of the disaster.

On the banks of the Little Big Horn, Custer and his two hundred and eleven troopers died to a man. Not one lived to tell the story of Custer's last stand.

troops were to go with Major Reno who, although recommended three times for gallantry in action during the Civil War, was not experienced in Indian fighting. Three troops were to accompany Captain Benteen, an older officer who disliked Custer intensely. The twelfth and last troop was to guard the pack train. Some of his officers thought the regiment should not have been split up without the support of Terry's and Gibbon's troops.

The weary but gallant 7th swung into their saddles and moved off.

No soldier lived to tell the story of Custer's last stand. The records we have today have been told by Indian warriors and scouts who, years afterwards, related their experiences.

Custer, doubtless with a glint of war shining in his eyes, led his two hundred and eleven men in a wild charge over the ridge down into the valley below. Crazy Horse, Rain-in-the-Face, and Gall were waiting and ready for the attack. Uttering piercing war cries, hundreds of warriors swarmed around Custer and his men from all sides.

In one brief, terrifying hour it was all over.

The white soldiers were mown down by the Indians' repeater rifles. Desperately the soldiers fired their single-shot Springfields until

they became red hot. The soft cartridge cases jammed in the breeches, as they had been known to do. Many a trooper died while frantically trying to dig out the cases with his knife. The unfortunate troopers never stood a chance against the modern Winchester repeating rifles the Indians were using.

The Sioux and Cheyennes, their faces frighteningly smeared with war paint, fought viciously against the hated white soldiers. For once they had the advantage over them. Repeaters spat, and spiked war clubs rose and fell, smashing the skulls of the soldiers. Dead horses lay all round them.

Custer made his last stand near the summit of a hill, his men grouped around him. He stood there bravely blazing away with his revolver. Within a short time all the ammunition had been used up. The last cartridges had been fired from the red hot carbines. The few men left standing with their commander were killed even as they emptied their revolvers into

The soldiers never stood a chance against the horde of Indian warriors.

Lieutenant Colonel Custer with his wife (seated on his right), his brothers, Boston (in top hat seated on left) and Tom (on right with sombrero and white neckerchief). Standing on Custer's right is Myles Keogh, whose horse Comanche was the only survivor of the massacre.

the hordes of warriors milling round them.

Suddenly, two bullets hit Custer, one in the head and the other in his side. He fell headlong to the ground, surrounded by his dead troopers.

A horrific sight met General Terry and Colonel Gibbon on the morning of June 27. The battlefield was strewn with the bodies of the two hundred and eleven men and their impetuous commander. Many had been scalped and stripped of their uniforms. As the two officers picked their way through the field of dead soldiers and horses they found Custer's body. He had not been scalped.

For a long time the Indians had wanted the scalp of Yellow Hair to add to their collection of trophies. Before setting out on the march, Custer had suddenly decided to have his long hair cut so that he was not recognized by the warriors. It was much later that they learned Yellow Hair had fought there that day.

Through his complete disregard of orders, Custer had unnecessarily sacrificed the lives of his troops, including four of his relatives. His two brothers, Boston and Tom, who was Captain of C Troop (he had been twice awarded the Medal of Honor in the Civil War), his nephew, Henry Armstrong Reed, and his brother-in-law, Lieutenant James Calhoun of L Troop, were all killed on that fatal day.

Captain Benteen and Major Reno had fought bravely and well and were later given promotions. Forty-seven of Reno's men had been killed and fifty-three wounded.

There was just one survivor of that terrible battle. It was Comanche, a beautiful charger that belonged to Captain Myles Keogh, a pleasant, laughing Irish officer, liked by all his **fellow officers and men. Comanche was severely wounded and was found standing over** the dead body of its master. The faithful horse was taken away and looked after. In time it recovered from its wounds, but it was never ridden again, except on ceremonial occasions. It died at the age of 28 in 1891.

What a story the horse could have told if only it could have talked.

SOLDIERS OF THE FRONTIER

The men who manned the lonely army posts on the frontier were volunteers. They came from all walks of life. Some wanted excitement and glory; others wanted to travel and see the West. There were those who wanted to escape from working on farms and those who needed a job. Some volunteers were criminals avoiding capture who changed their names. Some were immigrants from Europe who could barely speak English. Men joined up for every reason under the sun.

The life the volunteers chose was hard, tough, and often brutal.

Soldiers out on campaigns spent hours in the saddle or on foot, always alert, ready to grab their carbines at the first sign of Indians. Revolvers nestled in holsters on their right hips, and sheath knives hung from their belts.

Sabers were usually left behind at the garrison. A surprise night attack could be spoiled by their telltale "clanking," a sure sign of approaching soldiers. Sabers were cumbersome weapons, but many a cavalryman, fighting for his life, wished his saber was at hand when his ammunition had given out and he was engaged in hand-to-hand combat with the enemy.

Infantrymen, too, left their bayonets behind, preferring to use their knives when their guns became useless.

Army rations were poor. "Forty miles a day on beans and hay" was a favorite joke. In those days there were no trained cooks. Most of the men who prepared the meals knew nothing about cooking. Another joke among the men was that the cooks killed more soldiers than the Indians did. Beans, hardtack, greasy salt pork, and coffee formed their staple diet.

Soldiers had to survive and fight in appalling weather conditions, from freezing blizzards and deep snow to merciless heat and burning sun. In the early years of the Frontier Army, the uniforms were not warm enough to keep out the intense cold. In the summer heat, the same uniforms were too hot.

Men in the Indian-Fighting Army had many duties besides fighting battles against the warring Indian tribes. Troops were sent throughout the vast territory of the west from the Mississippi River to the Pacific Ocean. They protected miners, settlers, and cattle ranchers. They surveyed railroad lines and guarded the construction crews, since there was always the threat of an Indian attack. They escorted and protected wagon trains and kept the main trails or routes open and free of war parties. They built bridges and repaired telegraph lines, which the Indians called "whispering wires" and frequently pulled down. The soldiers did any job that was required of them and did it well.

Some of the most reliable soldiers were black. They served in four regiments under white officers. They fought hard, seldom deserted, and were well disciplined. The Indians they fought respected them and called them "Buffalo Soldiers." They saw a resemblance between the curly hair of the black soldiers and the buffalo's shaggy coat. The Plains Indians considered the buffalo a sacred animal and were honoring the black soldiers by giving them that name.

Discipline in the Frontier Army was harsh. Men who committed small offenses such as oversleeping and missing roll call were fined a month's pay or

Army rations were poor. In this photograph, four troopers make the best of a meal of beans and salt pork washed down with scalding hot coffee.

General

Lieutenant Colonel

Sergeant

Private

confined to the guardhouse for a month – or both.

General Custer was particularly severe with the men under his command. He designed a special guardhouse. It was a 15-foot deep hole in the ground covered with boards. Soldiers imprisoned down there for minor offenses must have felt their punishment was very harsh indeed.

A soldier found drunk or disorderly might have been ordered to march all day, in all weathers, carrying a 30- to 40-pound log. If a soldier deserted and was captured, he would have to wear a 25-pound ball and chain around his ankle for weeks or even months, like a convict in a chain gang.

This sort of punishment was responsible for the desertion of a third of all the soldiers recruited during the Indian wars. Many wished they had not been so eager to volunteer.

Soldiers normally spent half their time on campaigns against the Indians and the rest of the time at an army post. They were glad to have a rest from long marches and fighting, but there were no home comforts in a fort.

In the 1860s forts or army posts were built of whatever material was available, usually wood, adobe, or logs mixed with sand, mud, and lime. To protect the garrison from sudden Indian attacks, since danger was never far away, high fences made of strong wooden stakes surrounded the buildings. These fences were called palisades or stockades. The fort gates were shut and barred at night, and sentries were posted along the top of the stockade. People living inside the enclosed fort felt safe and protected.

A fort had to have enough water for a regiment or several companies and grass for the horses. It usually contained a barracks, storehouses, stables, workshop, guardhouse, officers' quarters, married quarters, and a parade ground. Some forts had a blacksmith and a trading post.

A few officers and enlisted men were allowed to have their wives and children with them. The quarters where the soldiers and their wives lived was known as "Suds Row" or "Sudsville," because some of the wives did the laundry for the garrison. For this work they were paid from two to five dollars a month. Washing was hard work, but the "laundry ladies," as they were called, were only too pleased to earn a few dollars to supplement their husbands' pay. Soldiers were poorly paid.

The fort was a busy place. Bugle calls sounded all through the day, summoning the men to various duties. These included drills on the parade ground, barracks inspection, and guard duty. Horses had to be groomed, watered, and exercised. Men were detailed to cut wood for fuel and to bring in water. The parade ground had to be swept and the buildings kept clean. While these and other duties were being carried out, the soldiers always had to stay on the alert for any sudden attack by a war party.

Some of the small army camps scattered across the Plains were made of log huts and tents. These were usually infested with rats, mice, and insects. Living conditions in the small camps were even rougher than in the larger forts.

Whether in a large camp or small, it was a tough life for an army man on the frontier.

IN THE DAYS OF THE SOLDIERS

1754-1763	The French and Indian War gives Great Britain the advantage in North America.
1769	James Watt invents the first steam engine.
1773	The Boston Tea Party.
1774	The Minutemen are organized. They are pro-independence soldiers who are trained to fight the British at a minute's notice.
1775	The battle of Lexington and Concord begins the Revolutionary War.
1776	The Declaration of Independence is signed, formalizing the American commitment to freedom.
1783	The Treaty of Paris ends the Revolutionary War.
1789	George Washington, hero of the Revolution, becomes the first president.
1789	Inspired by America's successful war for independence, revolution breaks out in France.
1812-1814	Britain tries to regain her lost American colonies, resulting in the War of 1812.
1815	The Treaty of Ghent ends the War of 1812.
1823	President James Monroe formulates the Monroe Doctrine which states that the western hemisphere is no longer open to European colonization.
1836	Texas wins independence from Mexico with the Battle of the Alamo.
1852	Harriet Beecher Stowe writes Uncle Tom's Cabin.
1854	Passage of the Kansas-Nebraska Act increases tensions on the slavery issue.
1854	Abraham Lincoln and Stephen Douglas debate the issue of slavery.
1859	John Brown's raid on Harper's Ferry.
1861	Lincoln is elected president on an anti-slavery platform.
1861	Confederate troops attack Fort Sumter, beginning the Civil War.
1861	The Battle of Bull Run. Northern troops are defeated. General Robert E. Lee distinguishes himself and becomes leader of the Confederacy.
1863	Lincoln issues the Emancipation Proclamation, freeing the slaves.
1864	General Ulysses S. Grant becomes chief of northern forces, later he will become president.
1865	In April, Lee surrenders to Grant at Appomattox, ending the Civil War.
1865	Lincoln is assassinated in Ford's Theatre by John Wilkes Booth.
1865	The Thirteenth Amendment to the Constitution abolishes slavery.
1870	The Fifteenth Amendment to the Constitution gives blacks the right to vote.
1890	Begun in 1861, the Apache Wars finally end with the defeat of the Indian tribe.
1890	After decades of fighting, the Sioux Wars end. Much blood has been shed on both sides.